D0952668

GUIDEPOSTS

"While Shepherds Washed Their Flocks"

"While Shepherds Washed Their Flocks"

And Other Funny Things Kids Say and Do

Liz Curtis Higgs

AN ENCOURAGER®

Illustrated by Dennis Hill

Carmel, New York 10512

This Guideposts edition is published by special arrangement with Thomas Nelson Publishers.

www.guideposts.org

The Bible version used in this publication is THE NEW KING JAMES VERSION. Copyright © 1979, 1980, 1982, 1990, Thomas Nelson, Inc., Publishers.

Library of Congress Cataloging-in-Publication Data

Higgs, Liz Curtis.
    While shepherds washed their flocks and other funny things kids say and do / Liz Curtis Higgs ; illustrated by Dennis Hill.
      p.   cm.
    ISBN 0-7852-7613-0
    1. Children—Quotations. 2. Children—Humor. I. Title.
PN6328.C5H49   1998
081'.083—dc21

                                      98-27249
                                        CIP

Printed in the United States of America.

On behalf of the hundreds of
mothers, grandmothers,
aunts, and educators
represented here, this
book is dedicated to
all our children.

You know who you are.

Contents

Acknowledgments

Heartfelt thanks to the hundreds of women who found a moment in their busy lives to share their stories with me by post, fax, or e-mail. Bless you for your generosity. (Yes, I agree—your children are adorable!)

Hugs of gratitude to my official readers and graders, who carefully reviewed each story and gave me priceless feedback and direction:

Lila Empson, Freelance Editor and Grandmother of Two
Sara Fortenberry, Literary Agent and Stepmother of Two
Shannan Giyer, Early Childhood Educator and Mother of One
Bill Higgs, Director of Operations, Father of Two, and Handsome Hubby
Mary Lee Higgs, Retired English Teacher and Mother-in-Law Superior

Jackie Jackson, Retired Kindergarten Teacher and
   Grandmother of Three
Gloria Looney, Awesome Office Assistant and Grandmother
   of Nine
Diane Mansfield, Children's Minister and Mother of Three
Jo-Ann Taylor, Middle School Librarian and Mother of Two
Anita Wells, Christian Bookseller and Grandmother of Three
Kathy Wolfe, Miss Kentucky 1980 and Mother of Three

A dozen rolls of fax paper to artist and friend Dennis Hill
of Texas, who embodies the heart of a child and the talent of a
master. What a delight to work with you again, kind soul!
   Finally, my sincere thanks to you for opening this book. May
childlike faith, hope, and joy leap into your heart when you least
expect it.

"While Shepherds Washed Their Flocks"

GUESS WHAT JUNIOR SAID TODAY?

Every mother, and especially every grandmother, thinks her offspring are hysterically funny. "You'll never believe what our four year old said," a woman in Topeka assures me.

Oh, I'll believe it, all right. Preschoolers are liable to say anything. I've raised two of them, and wished I'd kept a pencil handy to record every one of their amazing utterances.

Alas, despite our best intentions, those kid-size quotable quotes are usually shared with family members, friends, or coworkers at the first opportunity, quickly replaced by some new amusing thing, never to be mentioned again.

Except the really juicy ones.

Those are the memorable stories told at every family gathering, embellished with so many details as to become apocryphal, woven into the fabric of a family's oral tradition. Such are the gems you'll find here, stories recorded on the tablets of a mother's or grandmother's heart, hidden in the memory banks of an observant teacher, or tucked in the apron pocket of a kind neighbor.

Because I'm an organized person (though admittedly, only on paper), like-minded stories are grouped together here by topics, each one introduced with my own musings on life with Lillian and Matthew and Bill (he's the other adult at our house).

Like my own children, the ones quoted here are honest (sometimes painfully so), verbally courageous (or is that outrageous?), wildly imaginative, and very funny indeed.

For the laughs that follow, we owe them all an affectionate squeeze of gratitude. Thanks, little ones, for allowing us to peek over your shoulders at an innocent world we'd almost forgotten.

1

OUTDOOR ADVENTURES

Bill and I not only don't play sports, we don't even watch them. Imagine our surprise when we produced two kids who want to attend every sports camp on the agenda.

We installed a basketball backboard so Matthew can teach us to shoot hoops. We're marking out Tuesday and Friday nights for the next decade so we can warm up the bleachers in the gym. We're buying extra health insurance and practicing our first aid skills.

We're almost ready for recreational action. Got any ibuprofen?

"While Shepherds Washed Their Flocks"

Little League baseball rolled around again, and someone asked two boys what positions they planned to try out for.

"Shortstop," the oldest one declared.

Just as quickly, his younger brother replied, "I'm trying out for the shade."

— Sandra from Mississippi

A young boy in the neighborhood was excitedly describing his first airplane ride.

"Boy, I bet you had a ball!"

"Nope," the little boy replied. "But I had a bat once."

— Priscilla from Kentucky

One evening after an especially close and tiring Little League game that the team lost by one run, the kids trudged off the field.

Trying to encourage them, their coach insisted, "No matter what happens, you'll always be winners with me!"

From the back of the line a voice said, "That's because you run too slow, Coach."

— *Ellen from Pennsylvania*

"While Shepherds Washed Their Flocks"

To get her grandson's mind off his upcoming tonsillectomy, Martha took the seven year old fishing. As she struggled to wrestle the hook out of the mouth of a small sunfish, her grandson's eyes widened with horror.

"Is that what it will be like when they take out my tonsils?"

— *Martha from Indiana*

Two boys, four and five, rode by a water reservoir. The younger one said, "Now, that would be a good place to swim!"

The older and naturally wiser one promptly responded, "Oh no! We can't swim in there—it's too dirty. We drink that water."

— *Beth from California*

Outdoor Adventures

Six-year-old Jordan had just visited Washington, D.C., and was enthralled by the history of his country, especially the Civil War.

One night as his family discussed their discoveries, Jordan turned to his grandfather and politely inquired, "Grandpa, were you in the war?"

"Yes, son, I was."

Jordan became very excited. "Which side did you fight for—the North or the South?"

— Jan from Rhode Island

Preparing to go through customs *en route* to Niagara Falls, Debra and her husband told their children that they'd be stopped before entering Canada. "We'll tell them we're staying two nights, and that we brought only our suitcase full of clothes."

Their six year old asked, "When we go home, will we say 'dirty clothes'?"

— Debra from Ohio

A father was trying to prepare his daughter Katelyn, three, for the long trip to Disneyland. Idaho to California is a difficult concept for a toddler.

"The car ride to see Mickey Mouse will be really, really l-o-n-g," he explained.

"That's okay," she assured him. "We can just ride our bikes."

— *Allison from Idaho*

"While Shepherds Washed Their Flocks"

Andrew was going on and on about a balloon ride he was planning to take with his cousins. "I've already got my ticket," he said proudly.

"What ticket?" his mother asked him, perplexed. "What are you talking about? What balloon ride?"

He pointed to the House for Sale sign in a neighbor's yard, which featured the RE/MAX logo—a hot air balloon—and a display of flyers about the house.

"See, Mom?" Andrew said confidently. "That's where I got my ticket!"

— *Jamie from Indiana*

Outdoor Adventures

While the family was decorating their front porch for Christmas, three-year-old Emily noticed that all the leaves had fallen off the Japanese maple in the yard. She asked, "Do you want me to hang those leaves on the tree?"

—*Mary Ann from Arkansas*

Vicky's two boys had been fighting most of the day and she'd had enough. She sent them outdoors with instructions to "play nicely until I call you in."

Half an hour later, she looked out the kitchen window and couldn't see them. Her heart stopped. She ran to the door, only to spy them perched on the neighbor's back porch, each with a big, fresh chocolate chip cookie in hand.

As Vicky leaned out the door, she heard her five year old tell their neighbor, "Mom sent us outside because we were driving her nuts!"

—*Vicky from Washington*

2
IS *THAT* HOW IT WORKS?

Listening to children on the phone is always an education. Their early conversations are short and disjointed, but the chattier ones soon learn to love Ma Bell.

I recently heard Lillian call up a friend, only to learn from the girl's mother that she was out for the afternoon.

"Oh my," Lillian sighed. "When will she be back?"

Clearly it was going to be many hours later, and the mother must have asked Lillian if she wanted to leave a message. This was a new concept for her.

"A message?" Lillian said, dumbfounded. "Well . . . tell her to put my foot in her prayers."

A big "haaawwww!" slipped out of my mouth before I could

stop it. (I've heard of putting your foot in your mouth, but in your prayers?)

"Mo-ther!" Lillian whined, stamping her foot. The same foot she'd supposedly hurt a week earlier, the one with the Ace bandage, the one that she'd danced on seconds ago without so much as a wince.

She returned to her phone conversation with a sniff. "Tell Morgan to put my foot in her prayers and I'll call back later." At which point, she might throw in the other foot to keep things hopping.

Kids not only have to sort out their own language discrepancies, they also spend their first decade discovering what in the world *we* are talking about.

Five-year-old Kayla was interested in her grandmother's antique shoehorn. Kayla inspected it carefully then asked, "How do you make it honk?"

— *Dorothy from Pennsylvania*

"While Shepherds Washed Their Flocks"

Kevin, three, and his grandma noticed a wasps' nest near her front door. She got the insect spray, and cautioned Kevin to move away. "This isn't good for you."

Kevin watched her spraying and the wasps falling to the ground. "I don't think it's very good for *them* either!"

— *Jenifer from Minnesota*

Miranda, three, was helping her grandpa do chores around the house. Soon she grew weary of the tasks. "Grandma," she sighed, "how much longer do we have to put up with him?"

— *Monica from Arizona*

Grandmother was reading three-year-old Elizabeth a book of famous sayings, including "Diamonds are a girl's best friend."

"But, Grandma," Elizabeth protested. "I thought *boys* were."

— *Elizabeth from Kentucky*

"While Shepherds Washed Their Flocks"

Elaine was attending a convention and brought her family with her. Each day, she got up quietly and sneaked out since her husband and son didn't need to get up so early.

One morning, as soon as she shut the door, her five year old ran around to her side of the bed and exclaimed in dismay, "Oh no! She got away again!"

— *Elaine from Washington*

An eight-year-old boy received something he'd always wanted—bunk beds—and, of course, he wanted to sleep on the top bunk. The first night, he fell off. The second night, he fell off again.

On the third night, when his mother tiptoed into his room to kiss him goodnight, she discovered that he'd used his toy sheriff kit to handcuff himself to the bars.

— *Tess from Texas*

Is *That* How It Works?

When Aubrey was four, her father asked her if she wanted to help him rake leaves. Out to the backyard they went, where the ground was full of colorful leaves.

He gave her a small rake to use, which she held up high in the air, pointing it toward the leaves still on the tree. "Daddy," she cried in frustration, "I can't reach them."

—*Wendy from Illinois*

A teacher asked her kindergarten class, "Why do we wear rings on our fingers instead of wearing them on our toes?"

Five-year-old Paige said confidently, "I know why. When the bride walks down the aisle and it's time for the ring, she'd have to take off her shoe."

Another student chimed in, "Yeah, and her pantyhose too!"

—*Jackie from Kentucky*

"While Shepherds Washed Their Flocks"

Three-year-old Claire was in time-out . . . again. Sensing that the girl was not standing properly, her mother marched in and gave her strict instructions: "Turn around and put your nose in the corner."

"But, Mom," she whined, "my nose won't fit!"

—*Lynett from Arkansas*

3

GROWTH SPURT

Whenever we visit family, they marvel at our children and exclaim, "My, how they've grown!" Let's face it, that's what kids do best.

We parental types have grown right along with them. Our kids have taught us how to help another person blow his nose (no easy trick, this), how to eat sparingly (only brown food is edible), how hard it is to tie shoelaces upside down and backward, and how meaningful a hug is when you really love the huggee.

They've also given us a new spin on aging—pardon me, maturing—and helped us accept the fact that everyone on the planet is growing older at exactly the same rate—one day at a time.

"While Shepherds Washed Their Flocks"

Lindy, four, was boasting to her grandparents, "I'm growing and growing!" She pointed toward the floor. "See how long my legs are? They're as long as my trousers!"

— *Lehrene from Washington*

When Reide was two, his parents taught him the names of his grandparents. He did very well with everyone's name except one grandmother—Shirlye.

Reide frowned and shook his head. "I can't say that. My teeth are too young."

— *Brenda from Indiana*

At age three, Elaine's son informed her, "Now, I'm a boy, but I'm going to grow up to be a teenager!"

— *Elaine from Washington*

Growth Spurt

Nathan, three, was trying to figure out how his older brother Eric and Eric's friend, Greg, could both be five and not have the same birthday.

"Eric is five and three-quarters," Greg's mother explained.

Thinking for a moment, Greg added, "Yeah, and Nathan is three and two dimes!"

— Joanne from Indiana

A woman let her hair color grow out farther than usual and the gray was shining through. When she finally visited her beautician, she walked out with fresh color and much shorter hair.

A five-year-old friend saw her new hairdo. "Wow, you got your hair cut!" he exclaimed. Then he turned around and looked again. "And they painted it too!"

— Mary Jo from Kentucky

"While Shepherds Washed Their Flocks"

When her grandparents arrived in Montana for their annual summer visit, their three-year-old granddaughter jumped in her granddaddy's lap and stared at his bald scalp.

"Oh, Grandpa," she moaned. "The Indians got your hair!"

— *Joan from Mississippi*

One-year-old David sat at the dinner table with his parents. He patted his own head and said, "Hair, hair." He reached up and patted his mother's head. "Hair, hair."

Then he patted his father's bald head and said, "Uh-oh."

— *Jackie from Kentucky*

Diane was combing out the tangles in her three-year-old son's hair.

"Ouch, Mommy!" he said. "I've got wrinkles in my hair!"

— *Diane from Indiana*

"While Shepherds Washed Their Flocks"

Kayla, eight, was trying to teach her sister Haley, four, how to curtsy. As she demonstrated, Haley asked in amazement, "Who taught you how to curtsy?"

Kayla replied, "Mom did."

"But who taught Mom how to curtsy?" Haley persisted.

"Her aunt and mother did."

"Well who taught them how to curtsy?"

Exasperated, Kayla blurted out, "The dinosaurs!"

— *Bonnie from Missouri*

4

MIND YOUR MANNERS

It's dangerous when you have your "good" child first. The compliant, obedient, lives-to-please-his-mother child. The sleeps-through-the-night, no-hassle, quiet child. You begin to think there really isn't much to parenting after all. Just feed 'em, change 'em, hug 'em—ta-da!

Watching children misbehave in church, we'd shake our heads with a hint of superiority, thinking to ourselves, "Their mother really doesn't know what she's doing, poor dear."

Then God gave us the child we deserve. A real kid, one who whines, refuses to eat vegetables, tests our authority at every turn, and in general, expands the definition of the Terrible Twos.

That same child has stolen our hearts as completely as the first one. With all that bravado comes an impressive dose of courage. Each emotional cloudburst produces a rain of kisses and hugs that are hard to resist. From an artistic temperament blooms breathtaking artistic ability.

Okay, so they're different. That's what makes parenting interesting.

Disciplining children is decidedly not a "one-style-fits-all" affair. With the first child, a single raised eyebrow straightens him up immediately. With our second child, it takes both eyebrows, many words, a time-out or two, and a big dose of patience—on her part.

Making them mind their manners is mostly "mind over matter"—if you don't mind, it won't matter!

Mind Your Manners

Robin had prepared a new recipe for dinner that her daughters wouldn't touch. Three-year-old Macy finally asked, "Mommy, do you like it?"

"Yes, I do."

Macy pushed her plate away. "Here, you can have mine!"

— *Robin from Indiana*

Paula tried to limit her children's intake of soda pop, especially the kind with caffeine. When her three-year-old daughter, Brooke, asked for a sip, Paula explained, "No, it will keep you awake."

When Brooke saw her mother drinking a soda with "caffeine-free" on the can, she brightened up. "Mommy, now can I have some of your pop? I promise it will make me stay in bed!"

— *Paula from Nebraska*

"While Shepherds Washed Their Flocks"

A four-year-old girl and her younger brother were in their family room, jumping from the couch to the floor. Their daddy told them, "Stop that! You could get hurt."

As the parents listened from the kitchen, they heard their daughter proclaim in her preschool, know-it-all voice, "Come on, let's jump. Daddy doesn't spank very hard."

— *Miriam from Indiana*

At Cyndi's house, it's a family rule to ask to be excused from the dinner table before getting up. When her son was five, he asked his daddy for permission to leave the table. His father was involved in conversation and didn't hear the request.

A little impatiently, the boy asked again. His father still did not hear. A third time. Still no response.

In exasperation he looked toward heaven and said, "Jesus, may I please be excused?"

— *Cyndi from Kentucky*

Mind Your Manners

Phoebe, three, was misbehaving in the car. When they stopped at the grocery store, her mother explained that because Phoebe had acted up, there would not be a treat.

Holding her mother's hand as they walked into the store, Phoebe announced, "Mom, I can read that sign up there."

"Really?" Her surprised mother waited to hear K-R-O-G-E-R.

"Yup. That sign says, 'Phoebe is a good girl and should get a treat today!'"

— *Pamela from Pennsylvania*

Abby, four, was trying to master eating spaghetti with a fork instead of with her fingers. "You need to learn to eat like a lady," her mother insisted. "Someday you may eat dinner with the president, or a king, or a queen."

Abby sighed. "I'd rather eat with Mr. Rogers."

— *Linda from Oregon*

"While Shepherds Washed Their Flocks"

It was bedtime and four-year-old Emily complained that she wasn't ready to go to sleep. Her mother explained that when Emily was born, God gave her mother the job of taking care of her, making sure she ate right and got enough sleep to stay healthy.

"I'm not trying to be mean," her mother assured her, "but this is the job that God gave me."

Emily declared, "Then you're fired!"

— *Sharon from Pennsylvania*

Angela's three-year-old daughter would do anything to delay her nap. After putting her daughter to bed one day, Angela heard noises coming from the girl's room and went in to find her standing on the windowsill.

"What are you doing?" Angela demanded.

"I'm waiting for Peter Pan to come take me away."

— *Angela from Oklahoma*

Mind Your Manners

Cynthia and Greg have different disciplinary styles. He's the softie, she's the tough one. Boone, two, was not happy with his mother's no-nonsense methods and kept calling, "Daddy! Daddy!"

Cynthia said sternly, "Do *not* say Daddy again."

Boone took a deep breath and tried another approach. "Greg! Greg!"

— *Cynthia from Kentucky*

Susanne taught her boys that when they played a game, the loser should always congratulate the winner.

Benjamin, three, was soundly beating Jonathan, six, in one round of Uno after another. Finally, Susanne prompted, "Now, Jonathan, what do you say to your brother?"

"Do-do-head," he retorted.

"Jonathan!" Susanne gasped.

"Uh—that's Spanish for 'congratulations!'"

— *Susanne from Kentucky*

"While Shepherds Washed Their Flocks"

Rodney and his older sister Frances were playing outside in their bare feet one summer night. When bedtime rolled around, their father told Rodney to scrub his feet before he climbed under the covers. "Those feet are filthy!" his dad insisted.

A few minutes later, Rodney showed up for inspection. "How do they look?" he wanted to know.

"Fine, son, but you're going to get your feet dirty all over again by walking around without your slippers."

"No problem," Rodney assured him. "I didn't wash the bottoms."

— *Frances from Arkansas*

Mind Your Manners

Florence's eight-year-old neighbor stopped by for a visit. The conversation that day revolved around his older brother's birthday.

"My brother is twenty-four. How old are you?" he wanted to know.

A little stunned, Florence replied, "Ladies don't tell their age as a rule."

"That's okay," he said. "I got it figured out."

"Ohh?"

"With all that gray hair, you must be about ninety."

Since she was only in her fifties, she said with a twinkle in her eye, "Well, you're wrong, and I'm still not going to tell you my age."

It was his turn to be shocked. "Golly, are you older than ninety?!"

—Florence from Kansas

5
FOUR-LEGGED FRIENDS

We are cat people. I've had a cat in my life more years than not. When I was nine, Tiger purred her way into my heart, to be followed by Max, Big Cat, Sassy, and now Leona (commonly known as "the slug on the rug").

I'm allergic to cats, of course, but I never let a sneeze get between me and my furry friends. Our kids are equally smitten with kittens, a fact that makes it easier to keep a cat around every time hubby steps over the sleeping fourteen-pound feline and grumbles, "Tell me again the purpose of this animal?!"

Yes, cats sleep sixteen hours a day, and bathe for another. Yes, they need expensive shots and flea medicine and special brushes and clean litter boxes. Often.

We've also had as many as eleven gerbils in captivity at

once—all named after U.S. presidents. Life was not always calm at 1600 Gerbil Avenue, however. Jefferson kept eating Lincoln's pellets, and while Washington was busy refereeing, Adams hogged the water bottle. Poor Buchanan, the bachelor president, passed away one chilly winter night, and we soon discovered that Adams wasn't John Quincy but rather Jane Quincy, who gave birth to Taft, Roosevelt, and Eisenhower.

Kids and animals make likely bedfellows. Both need endless care and feeding, yet the moment you entertain thoughts of finding them a new home, they look up at you with adoring eyes and drop today's newspaper at your feet.

Okay, you can stay. Forever.

Four-Legged Friends

Christine was rehearsing her first oral report for kindergarten. She suddenly stopped, pointed to her cat poster, and asked, "Do you know how you can tell a girl kitty from a boy kitty?"

Her parents held their breath.

"A girl kitty has long eyelashes."

— Jo-Ann from Kentucky

Danny, four, moved to a cattle ranch with his family. They ventured into the barn to see a calf being born. Danny asked, "Is it a boy or a girl?"

The ranch manager flipped the animal over. "It's a boy!"

Later that evening Danny asked, "Mom, was it written on its foot that it was a boy?"

— Amy from Nebraska

"While Shepherds Washed Their Flocks"

A young boy was excitedly sharing about watching a deer cross the road right in front of his family's car. He added with amazement, "And it wasn't even at one of those 'Deer Crossing' signs!"

— *Betty from North Carolina*

"What's your new doggie's name?" Barbara asked three-year-old Hannah.

"Molly."

"Do you know what kind of dog Molly is?"

"Oh, yes!" Hannah assured her. "A basket hound."

— *Barbara from Pennsylvania*

"While Shepherds Washed Their Flocks"

One sunny day, Ellen's family gathered for lunch at a local park so they could admire the scenery while they ate. As a flock of geese came around the corner of the lake, four-year-old Jason exclaimed, "Daddy, look at all the gooses!"

His father, trying to teach Jason proper English, said, "One goose, many geese. Think of the word mouse. What do you say when there are many?"

Jason thought for a split second, then triumphantly said, "Minnie Mouse!"

— Ellen from Pennsylvania

Young Taylor was trying to coax a cat from the next yard to come and play with him.

"That kitty doesn't know you," his grandmother explained.

Taylor promptly held out his hand in the cat's direction. "Taylor here!"

— Priscilla from Kentucky

"While Shepherds Washed Their Flocks"

A farm couple hosted a tour of their dairy milk parlor, calf barn, and silo for their son's kindergarten class. A few weeks later, a little girl came running up to the mother at school.

"I know you!" she exclaimed.

"You do?"

"Sure. You're the Farmer in the Dell's wife!"

— Portia from Kentucky

Seth's mother was trying to get her young son to sing "Old MacDonald Had a Farm," but each time she mentioned an animal, he clamped his lips shut and shook his head. "No!"

Frustrated, she finally asked him, "Well, what does Old MacDonald have, Seth?"

He grinned. "French fries!"

— Karleen from Indiana

44

Four-Legged Friends

When Mike was three, he went with his parents to visit an aunt and uncle who lived on a big farm. Uncle Henry took Mike along to milk the cows.

It wasn't too long before Mike came running back in the house, bug-eyed. "Mama, Mama, guess what?" he exclaimed. "Uncle Henry's cow has a beach ball!"

—*Gloria from Kentucky*

6
MUMS AND DADS

Once you become a parent, there's no need to pray for humility—it's part of the job description.

And forget using your own name. You are now known as "the mother of—" or "the father of—." At PTO meetings, I'm greeted with, "Oh, you're Lillian's mother." The tone suggests they know something I don't.

"That's me!" I agree, genuinely proud of my daughter.

"So I see," they murmur and slip away with a sly smile.

My eyes become narrow daggers, aimed at the departing parent's back. "Aren't you the mother of Bridget the barbarian who bites the heads off her gingerbread men?!?" I mumble under my breath.

Sometimes a mother gets no respect from anyone, of any age.

"While Shepherds Washed Their Flocks"

There are other times, though, when our children toss crowns of glory at our feet. I won an award from my peers in professional speaking a few years back and brought the family with me to our gala awards banquet.

Since the identity of the five award recipients was a surprise to the sixteen hundred attendees, we had a trusted friend sit right outside the ballroom with our kids, dressed in their tuxedo-and-frilly-dress best, waiting until my name was announced.

Lillian took care of all that. As people streamed in, she called out in her loudest, proudest voice, "My mom is winning a big award tonight!"

Ah well. Who cares about the element of surprise? The joy shining in my daughter's eyes was enough. It makes up for many a too-honest comment like, "Gee, Mom, your tummy jiggles like Jell-O!"

Mums and Dads

Her father was attending a Promise Keepers conference, so five-year-old Nicollette and her mother went to church by themselves.

A friend inquired, "Nicollette, where's your daddy tonight?"

She proudly replied, "He's at Housekeepers!"

— *Dana from California*

Jerri and her husband always told their eight-year-old son that since he was their first child he was their guinea pig, and that although they would make mistakes, they'd learn from them.

"Didn't you take a class for this?" he asked, having watched his mother take one class after another for postgraduate studies.

"No, I didn't."

He looked at her very seriously. "Well, I think you should have!"

— *Jerri from Indiana*

"While Shepherds Washed Their Flocks"

One Sunday, Rae Ann was chatting about her husband, a minister, who would "soon be marrying Jane and Tom."

Their young son, overhearing the conversation, looked stricken. "Mom, aren't you and Dad going to be married anymore?!"

— *Rae Ann from Pennsylvania*

Kathy's mother was getting ready to head out the door, and told her daughter to mix a cake and get it in the oven.

"But, I don't know how!" Kathy whined.

"Just follow the directions on the box," her mother said. The young girl read the directions, scrubbed her hands thoroughly, dumped all the ingredients in the bowl, and started mixing.

When her mother came back to check on her, she found Kathy up to her elbows in batter. "What are you doing?!?"

"The directions said to mix the cake by hand."

— *Kathy from Indiana*

Christine quit her job to stay home and her coworkers gave her many gifts, including a recipe card holder that she really had no use for. Christine decided it would be a perfect gift for newlyweds, so she bought some recipe cards to put inside, wrapped it, and took it to a wedding shower at church.

Chloe, three, was sitting in her mother's lap when the bride-to-be opened their gift. In a loud voice, the little girl announced, "That used to be ours, but we didn't need it anymore!"

— *Christine from Texas*

As a parent educator, Stacy worked with a group of children learning their colors. One mother asked her little girl, "What does red mean?

The girl replied, "Stop."

"How about green?"

"That's Go." Before either of them could ask her, the girl added, "And yellow is Hurry Up, Hurry Up, Hurry Up—right, Mommy?"

— *Stacy from Kansas*

In an effort to comfort a little boy whose father had died, Carole asked him gently, "What were your father's last words?"

"He didn't have any. Mom was with him to the end."

— *Carole from Missouri*

Mums and Dads

Joyce overheard her children talking about being pretty, rich, and/or famous some day. Hoping to impress them that being nice and kind was more important, she asked, "Don't you know some people that are not so good-looking, but they're very nice?"

Her kids sat there stumped, until suddenly their oldest one said, "Yeah! You and Dad are nice, and you're not rich, famous, or good-looking!"

—Joyce from Montana

Pam spent an hour preparing for a much-needed night out with her husband. Finally, she sprayed on her favorite perfume, gave herself an approving nod in the mirror, and was feeling especially pretty until she stepped into the hallway and found her three-year-old daughter, Jenna, waiting for her.

"Mommy, you smell like carrots!"

—Pam from Nebraska

"While Shepherds Washed Their Flocks"

Beth was doing aerobics to *Kathy Smith's Workout* videotape. Her five-year-old son, watching her huff and puff, asked, "Mommy, why are you doing that?"

"Honey, I'm trying to lose some weight."

"He looked at Kathy Smith, then back at his mother, puzzled. "Well, *she* doesn't look like she needs to lose weight."

—*Beth from Minnesota*

Christopher, three, repeatedly asked his father why he had to go to work each morning. "Because, son, we need money to buy diapers and such."

The little boy understood and often repeated to anyone who would listen that his dad went to work to buy him diapers. When Christopher was finally potty trained, he proudly told his father, "Now you don't have to go to work anymore!"

—*Charlene from Virginia*

Mums and Dads

The neighborhood kids usually ended up in Alice's yard. One afternoon she heard fussing and crying, but when she investigated, no one would give her any answers.

Alice called over her five-year-old daughter and asked her to tell what happened. "Remember," Alice said, "Jesus knows what happened out there."

Her daughter grinned. "Yeah, but He can't tell you!"

—*Alice from Illinois*

7

DEEP QUESTIONS

Children are full of questions. "Why is the sky blue?" can be answered scientifically. "How many numbers are there?" can be answered mathematically.

"Where does a gerbil go when it dies?" is a toughie. "Into the ground" is a cop-out. "Dust to dust" is too scary a scenario, and spinning tales of "gerbil heaven" is bad theology.

When Mrs. Gerbil breathed her last, we had a good cry, all four of us. Lillian leaked first, of course, which set me off, which put Matthew under. When Bill returned from the burial mound, he found us all in a heap around the kitchen table and joined right in.

Some things are easy to explain. Other truths, as Bill would say, "aren't all nailed down." Come to think of it, I've known some people that weren't all nailed down either.

It may be those "loose boards" among us who can hit the nail on the head when it comes to answering life's toughest questions, though, especially if we answer truthfully, "Lord knows, child. Go ask your Father."

Deep Questions

When four-year-old Amanda smeared lipstick all over her face like a clown, her mother sighed and began to scrub it all off. "Tilt your head back, Amanda, so I can clean your forehead."

"Mommy, do I have a forehead?"

"Yes, you do."

Amanda thought for a minute. "Well, what number head do you have?"

— Betty from Pennsylvania

At bedtime, four-year-old Joshua and his mother, Debbie, were discussing what heaven would be like. Trying to put things in terms he would understand, Debbie explained, "In heaven, there won't be any more 'owies.'"

Joshua looked confused. "Why? Aren't there any sidewalks?"

— Debbie from Washington

"While Shepherds Washed Their Flocks"

Three-year-old Chip was looking through family photo albums with his two older sisters. Quite concerned, he asked his mother, "How come you took the girls to Disneyland without me?"

His mother tried to explain that the trip to the theme park occurred before he was born.

Chip looked up at her, wide-eyed. "You mean you went there when I was dead?"

— *Nancy from California*

"Mommy," a girl asked her mother one day, "how come when people get through praying, they always say 'Oh, man'?"

— *Jamie from Texas*

"While Shepherds Washed Their Flocks"

During a visit from her mother, Brenda convinced her to allow her three year old to brush her teeth at one sink while grandma used the other.

Reluctantly, her mother removed her dentures and began to clean them.

From outside the open bathroom door, Brenda heard her daughter say, "Granny, does your tongue come out too?"

— *Brenda from Delaware*

Hailey, five, was learning to read and had to painstakingly sound out each word out loud. She stopped and watched her mother reading silently to herself and asked, "Mom, how do you keep all of those words in your mouth?"

— *Cindy from Alaska*

8
BABIES AND OTHER STRANGERS

Children have no concept of what they were like as babies. You can show family videos of them screaming in their playpens and they'll disavow any knowledge of such activity.

On a recent family outing for pizza, we tried to politely ignore the folks in the next booth, whose infant son was wailing.

"Shhhhhh!" said the young mother, obviously distressed at the commotion.

When she could bear the incessant crying no more, our Lillian demanded a little too loudly, "Somebody turn down that baby!"

"While Shepherds Washed Their Flocks"

On their way to church one Sunday evening, a couple's six-year-old daughter blurted out, "Mommy, do you and Daddy have sex?"

Before they could say a word, their eight-year-old son shot back, "Of course not! They're good Christian people."

— *Jerri from Indiana*

Larry, age three, was playing with Lego plastic building blocks on the floor. He looked up at his father and innocently asked, "How do you make babies?"

His dad took a deep breath and plunged in, explaining that babies are a gift from God and that the Mommy and Daddy pray for a baby and God answers those prayers.

Larry patiently waited for him to finish. He sighed. "No, Daddy. How do you make babies out of Legos?"

— *Sandra from Virginia*

Babies and Other Strangers

When their second child arrived, the parents had a gift ready for six-year-old Eric, so he wouldn't be jealous of all the baby's presents.

The happy day arrived, and the proud father presented Eric with a copy of *James and the Giant Peach,* inscribed: "Dear Eric, I'm so glad to have you as my big brother. I love you, Scott."

Eric turned to his parents with a look of understanding on his face. "That explains it," he said.

"Explains what?" his father asked.

"Why he was in there so long. He had to write this whole book for me before he came out!"

— *Elizabeth from Colorado*

"While Shepherds Washed Their Flocks"

Wal-Mart was having a drawing for mothers-to-be to win baby merchandise. Since Gayle was expecting her fourth, she put her name in the box and explained to her three-year-old son that she was signing up for the baby and that they might win.

A few months later when she was preparing her children for what was going to take place and how Mommy would be in the hospital, her youngest chimed in confidently, "We're not getting our baby at the hospital. We're getting it at Wal-Mart!"

— *Gayle from Pennsylvania*

While visiting his grandmother, five-year-old Benjamin was looking at all the family photos. He was quiet for a moment, then said, "I like this family, and I like my family, but Grandma, why don't you have any children?"

— *Terri from Illinois*

Babies and Other Strangers

Judy's three-year-old niece went to Big Sister Class. When asked, "Would you like a little brother or a little sister?" the little girl responded, "I'd rather have a bunny."

— *Judy from Indiana*

Brooke, four, asked her grandparents for chewing gum. "Do you know what I do with my gum when I get done chewing it?"

They expected her to say, "Put it in the ashtray" or "Throw it out the window." Were they surprised when she answered, "I give it to my baby brother and he eats it!"

— *Paula from Nebraska*

"While Shepherds Washed Their Flocks"

When Will was two he didn't speak much and didn't have to since his older brother Andy, four, was happy to translate.

One evening at the dinner table, Will rattled off a string of syllables with great animation and expression.

"Andy, what did Will say?" his parents asked.

Andy immediately rattled off the same sounds.

"But what does that mean?" they asked.

"I don't know," Andy admitted. "He never said that before!"

— *Sue from Wisconsin*

Five-year-old Bradley knew all about animals, since his father was an avid hunter. When he saw toddler Elaine in her crib, he called out with glee, "Hey! She's standing on her hind legs!"

—*Kreta from Alaska*

Babies and Other Strangers

Devin was only five months old when his mother started babysitting Ariel. Now, at age three, he adored the little girl.

When Devin woke up from his nap, his mother told him, "Have I got a surprise for you! Ariel is coming over."

He sighed. "Does that mean it's time for us to get married?"

—*Rhonda from Indiana*

9

WORD PLAY

The English language is silly enough when used by adults who understand it. But in the hands of a still-learning child, words become magic tricks that turn sentences upside down.

Think of the hymn titles that have become more famous since traveling through a child's language center: "Gladly, The Cross-Eyed Bear" and "Hark! The Harold Angel Sings," to name two. A preschooler's verbal skills can only take him so far before his imagination takes over and fills in the blanks, with hilarious results.

"While Shepherds Washed Their Flocks"

Miriam's three-year-old granddaughter was riding in the back seat when she said, "Mamaw, I know how to spell umbrella."

Miriam was impressed. "You're looking at one behind my seat, aren't you? How do you spell umbrella?"

Her granddaughter answered with great care, "T-O-T-E."

— *Miriam from Indiana*

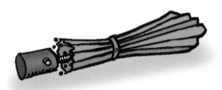

Paul, now nine, refuses to believe he ever said any of this, but when he was little he insisted that he wanted a "la-bore-a-dog retriever," the guy on the radio was a "renouncer," and his favorite dessert was "fruit cottontail"!

— *Janet from Texas*

Two-year-old Susie watched her grandfather sprinkling sugar on his cereal and exclaimed, "Snow!"

— *Barbara from Pennsylvania*

"While Shepherds Washed Their Flocks"

Randy loved to tell stories to the kids about "adventures" that he supposedly had with Winnie-the-Pooh. His niece, three, watched Uncle Randy telling his tall tales while an incredulous look spread across her face.

Finally she planted her fists on her hips and demanded to know, "Is this real, or is this fake-believe?"

— *Stephanie from Michigan*

Three-year-old Kate received a toy grocery checkout stand for Christmas. Her dad pinned the "Manager" tag on her. "You're ready to open your store now, Kate. You're the manager."

"But Daddy," she insisted, "I'm not a manager, I'm a ladyger!"

— *Marcia from Georgia*

"While Shepherds Washed Their Flocks"

One Fourth of July, seven-year-old Jonathan's aunt was rushed to the hospital with appendicitis. On the phone that night, Jonathan was filled with news about his aunt's interrupted holiday. "She had an operation!" he said excitedly. "She had to have her independence taken out!"

— Shirley from New York

Teenager Sarah told four-year-old Abby to pick up her toys. "First, Abby, put your marbles in a pile."

Abby declared, "I can't put them in a pile, but I can put them in a crowd."

— Linda from Oregon

Jacqueline's ten-year-old daughter waltzed into the kitchen while she was marinating steaks for dinner and said, "Oh, Mom, you're serenading the meat!"

— *Jacqueline from Illinois*

"While Shepherds Washed Their Flocks"

Five-year-old Ryan had a T-shirt depicting the planetary system. Since his family used to live on Jupiter Drive, the shirt was a helpful way for Ryan to remember the name of his street. After the family moved to another state, he still liked to wear the shirt because it brought back happy memories.

On a shopping trip one day, an elderly woman stopped Ryan and commented on his shirt. Brightening, Ryan exclaimed, "We used to live on Jupiter!"

The woman laughed. "Right, sonny, and I'm from Mars!"

— *Ellen from Pennsylvania*

Phyllis asked her three-year-old daughter if she wanted a scrambled egg.

"No way," she replied. "I want a together egg."

—*Phyllis from Michigan*

Young Neil's grandfather owned a heating and air-conditioning business, and Neil often heard him say, "Duct tape fixes everything."

When one of his toys broke, Neil headed for the workshop exclaiming, "Grampa, I need that goose tape!"

—*Maureen from Texas*

"While Shepherds Washed Their Flocks"

Three-year-old Matthew took a trip to visit his grandparents on their Mississippi farm. When they pulled up to the house, he said, "Where's the lady?"

"You mean Grandma?" his mother asked. "Inside the house, I suppose."

He shook his head. "No, the other lady."

"What other lady?"

"Miss Sippy."

—*Lawana from Louisiana*

10
SCHOOL'S IN

Notes from teachers, stuffed in backpacks, strike terror in a parent's heart. Did your child run his gym suit up the flagpole? Stuff his lunch down the principal's john? Tell his teacher that you drove him to school wearing your husband's pajamas?

Or worse, is there some assignment that's due within hours? A forgotten science project? A ten-page book report? Or—horrors!—a costume needed for tomorrow's school play?!?

I am sewing-impaired, so costumes do me in every time. "Can you staple fabric?" I wonder, panic rising in my throat. "Or would Scotch tape be safer? And what does a toad look like, anyway?"

When I'm the one making the costume, it looks like an old sheet dyed a yucky shade of olive, paired with green tights and Daddy's swim fins. In other words, awful.

"While Shepherds Washed Their Flocks"

We've decided the students who are really going to school are the parents. More than once, hubby and I have gazed at one another over the dessert plates and sighed. "So, do we have any homework tonight?"

School's In

It was time for five-year-old Hannah to go to kindergarten. Her school district did a prekindergarten test on each child, so her parents explained that she would go to school, meet the teachers, and answer some questions.

As she prepared for bed the night before, Hannah told her dad, "I need to get my backpack ready for tomorrow."

He assured her that she wouldn't need her backpack until fall.

"But I need it to take all the questions I'll ask *them*."

— *Carla from Missouri*

"While Shepherds Washed Their Flocks"

Jennifer went to the morning kindergarten class, which lasted from 9:00 to 11:40.

The following year she went to first grade, with classes from 9:00 until 3:15. After that long first day, she looked up at her mother and sighed, "So, how long do the *second* graders have to stay?"

— *Cindy from Nevada*

Four-year-old Jeffrey came home from preschool and proudly announced that he could count to one hundred, which he then proceeded to do.

"And what comes after one hundred?" his mother asked.
"Percent!"

— *Bev from California*

Shanna, a second-grader, informed her parents that she would have to study very hard because she had to memorize an important "declapendence."

Trying to keep a straight face, her mother asked her, "What is that you have to learn again?"

"You know, Mom, the Declapendence of Indapation!"

— *Betty from North Carolina*

After his first day of school, a little boy was asked what he'd learned that day. "Tissle tea," he said.

"Tissle what?" his mother asked, confused.

"You know, Mom. We learned how to sing, 'My Country, Tissle Tea.'"

— *Beatrice from Alabama*

"While Shepherds Washed Their Flocks"

In preparing her second-graders for a critical standardized test, Linda stressed the importance of listening and following all her directions.

The children began working, and as she casually strolled around she noticed Bobby working frantically over his paper. She was horrified to see he'd covered his test with huge check marks made with a bright red crayon.

"Bobby, what have you done?!" she gasped. "You've ruined your test!"

"No, ma'am." He calmly shook his head. "You told us to check every answer, so I did!"

— *Linda from Indiana*

When one child in kindergarten broke out with chicken pox, the teacher asked each child, "Have you ever had chicken pox?"

One boy said, "No, ma'am. But I've had goose bumps!"

— *Carolyn from Ohio*

Elaine asked her students to name the famous person in history who liked the flavor of saffron on his food.

One young boy answered promptly: "King Henry the Ape."

— *Elaine from Washington*

"While Shepherds Washed Their Flocks"

When Darrell was in kindergarten, he said me instead of I. After class one day, he said to his teacher, "Mrs. Frank, me can't put my coat on."

Mrs. Frank replied, "No, Darrell, I can't put my coat on, I can't put my coat on, I can't put my coat on."

Darrell shrugged. "That's okay, Mrs. Frank, me can't do it neither. Me go get Donna to do it for me."

— *Elizabeth from Kentucky*

Margaret asked her three-year-old granddaughter what she'd learned about that day.

She thought for a moment and said, "That man that built the wall. Uhm . . . Nehi . . . Nemi . . . Neosporin!" she shouted out proudly.

— *Margaret from Kentucky*

First-grader McNeil usually brought home a B+ or a B- grade on his school papers. When he discovered one marked with just a B, he exclaimed, "Look, Mom, I got a B nothing!"

—*Sandra from Mississippi*

11

HEAVENLY MATTERS

Mothers wonder if their children comprehend spiritual truths. God, heaven, life, death—do they get this stuff? All those flannelboards on Sunday mornings, all those hours at Vacation Bible School—are the stories sinking in, taking root, making a difference?

I decided to find out and so asked Lillian, "Who rules the universe?"

"God does!" she answered promptly.

"Very good. But what about Jesus?"

She pondered briefly then announced, "They work together."

"Oh? What about the Holy Spirit?"

"He works on weekends!"

Truer words were never spoken.

On the day Lillian was baptized, she was so excited she

practically dove into the baptistery, head first. I got wet, too . . . with tears. Such a happy, happy day.

Drying her off after the big event, I reminded her gently, "Now the Lord lives in your heart."

Lillian nodded enthusiastically. "I can feel Him rattling around in there already!" She suddenly pursed her lips tightly together, squeezing out the words like toothpaste. "Do I have to keep my mouth closed so He won't get out?"

Heavenly Matters

It was Palm Sunday and, because of strep throat, Sue's three-year-old son had to stay home from church with a babysitter. When the family returned home carrying palm branches, he asked what they were for.

"People held them over Jesus' head as He walked by," his mother explained.

"Wouldn't you know it," the boy fumed. "The one Sunday I didn't go, He showed up!"

— Sue from Kentucky

Two-year-old Jonathan came home after an exciting day at an amusement park. He enthusiastically described the carousel, the trains, and the bumper cars.

"The only thing I didn't like," he said with a frown, "was that Holy Ghoaster!"

— Pam from Pennsylvania

"While Shepherds Washed Their Flocks"

Two-year-old Caitlin was on a road trip with her grandmother and, because of construction, they missed their exit. Her grandmother prayed out loud, "Lord, help us find our way."

Within a mile, they spotted a police officer and asked him for directions. Driving away, grandmother prayed again, "Thank you, Lord, for taking care of us."

From the backseat, Caitlin's voice was filled with wonder: "Was that the Lord?"

— *Mary from Kansas*

Laurie, four, watched the rain pouring down until her curiosity got the better of her. "Is it raining so Jesus can have a drink?"

— *Lehrene from Washington*

"While Shepherds Washed Their Flocks"

Lisa had been sprinkled as a baby but wanted to be baptized by immersion at her new church. Her husband explained to their two-year-old daughter, Carrie, what baptism meant and why it was a special day for Mommy.

After the service the family went out to lunch to celebrate. A very prim and proper older woman came by the table and asked Carrie if she was dressed up for a special occasion.

"Oh, yes!" Carrie exclaimed. "The preacher threw Mommy in a big pot and washed all her skins away!"

— *Lisa from Virginia*

Cannon, three, was eager to show his mom what he learned in Sunday school. He pulled her over to the flannelboard with all the animals paired two by two.

"See, Mommy?" he said. "Here's Noah in the dark."

— *Shell from Indiana*

"While Shepherds Washed Their Flocks"

A group of children at church were singing the praise song "As the Deer Panteth for the Water." One little girl's voice was heard loudly above the others, "As the deer pants fall in the water . . ."

— *Deb from Colorado*

Andrea, five, was going through the Christmas catalog wanting this and that and the other. Her mother told her, "Okay, when our ship comes in, you can have it all."

Later her mom overheard Andrea telling her two sisters, "Did you all know we're getting a boat?"

— *Alice from Illinois*

At one school the second grade performed the Nativity scene every Christmas. Rehearsals started on the first day of school and were very intense.

One December day, Jeanne took her daughter to Radio City Music Hall to see the Christmas pageant. Throughout the performance her daughter oohed and aahed at the performers.

Finally she gasped, "Mommy, what a big second grade this school has!"

— *Jeanne from Pennsylvania*

Many Christmases ago, after the students finished singing "While Shepherds Watched Their Flocks by Night," one of the children commented, "Teacher, wasn't it nice of those shepherds to wash those sheep before taking them to Jesus?"

— *Beatrice from Alabama*

"While Shepherds Washed Their Flocks"

To celebrate the tradition of Saint Nicholas Day on December 6, the children in the family placed their shoes by the front door. During the night Saint Nicholas left treats and small gifts in their shoes.

Five-year-old Tom, who was really into watching golf on television and knew the names of all the pros, was up at the break of dawn that December 6 shouting, "Mom! Dad! Jack Nicklaus was here!"

— *Marilyn from Ohio*

When her son was five, Suzanne purchased a Christmas ornament shaped like a wreath, with a place for his photo in the center. As she placed the ornament on their tree, her young son looked at it in awe.

"Where did you get that, Mom?"

"I bought it at a little store down the street."

He stared at his photo in the center. "Um . . . are they selling very many of them?"

— *Suzanne from Kentucky*

"While Shepherds Washed Their Flocks"

One Christmas Eve, when Christine was five, a family friend asked her, "Have you been good all year?"

She replied emphatically, "Well, certainly not all year!"

— *Jo-Ann from Kentucky*

Sarah, three, was very interested in the Bible stories that her parents read to her each night. They often spoke of the Rapture and said how wonderful it will be to see Jesus someday.

One night before they turned off the lights, Sarah sat up in bed, looked her parents in the eye, and said, "You know this Rapture thing? Well, you and Daddy can go if you want to, but I'm going to Grandma's!"

— *Betty from North Carolina*

Heavenly Matters

One Easter, Kathy was explaining to her son Bob, age four, all the miraculous things that happened on Good Friday. Rather dramatically, she described how the sun went dark, the earth shook, and the dead walked around.

Bob got very quiet. Finally he asked, "Momma, was I taking a nap that day?"

—Kathy from Kentucky

Gloria's daughter was five when she saw a picture of Jesus with a golden halo circling His head. "Look, Mom," she said, wide-eyed, "Jesus has a hula hoop!"

—Gloria from Indiana

POST SCRIPT

Jesus said, "Whoever humbles himself as this little child is the greatest in the kingdom of heaven" (Matt. 18:4). May we all listen carefully, watch closely, and take detailed notes as the children in our lives teach us to embrace life with innocence, humility, and a childlike sense of humor.

Amen and "Oh, man!"

About the Author

Author and humorist Liz Curtis Higgs wears two hats with equal joy: writing encouraging books for young children and writing humorous books for adults. Her tenth book, *"While Shepherds Washed Their Flocks" and Other Funny Things Kids Say and Do,* brings those two joys together at last.

Liz's professional speaking career has spanned a dozen years and nearly all fifty states. Twelve hundred audiences in conference and retreat settings have laughed at her stories and applauded her encouraging messages since 1986.

Proud mother of two children, Matthew and Lillian, and happy wife of one husband, Bill, Liz celebrates life on Laughing Heart Farm in Louisville, Kentucky, with her family, three cats, and numerous gerbil rodentia.

Liz's free newsletter, *The Laughing Heart®*, is published twice a year and mailed to more than 17,000 readers worldwide. For your free copy, write:

> Liz Curtis Higgs
> PO Box 43577
> Louisville, KY 40253-0577

Other Great Books from Liz Curtis Higgs That Will Tickle Your Funny Bone

Help! I'm Laughing and I Can't Get Up!

Do you giggle, cackle, or whoop? Snort, chortle, or hoot? Celebrate the blessings and benefits of humor in our lives with this hilarious collection of stories from five hundred humor contributors. You'll also discover seven reasons why people laugh and Liz's four humor personalities — one of them will fit you to a tickled T!

ISBN 0-7852-7614-9 • Trade Paperback • 264 pages

Mirror, Mirror on the Wall, Have I Got News for You!

Liz serves up an encouraging alphabet soup of wisdom and humor for all of us who need a gentle reminder of how much we're valued by the One who made us. Previously published as *Reflecting His Image*, this 1997 paperback version now features uplifting cartoons and a colorful, zippy new look. Liz's favorite!

ISBN 0-7852-7109-0 • Trade Paperback • 144 pages

Forty Reasons Why Life Is More Fun After the Big 40!

Every woman from 39 to 99 will find something to laugh about in Liz's "forty - to-glory" book. Midlife stories from more than 400 women add to the fun, along with many humorous cartoons, zany 40th birthday celebrations and Liz's own joys and trials on the other side of the Big 4-0. All forty reasons are a hoot!

ISBN 0-7852-7615-7 • Trade Paperback • 252 pages

A Note From The Editors

This book was selected by the Book and Inspirational Media Division of the company that publishes *Guideposts*, a monthly magazine filled with true stories of people's adventures in faith.

Guideposts is not sold on the newsstand. It's available by subscription only. And subscribing is easy. All you have to do is write to Guideposts, 39 Seminary Hill Road, Carmel, New York 10512. When you subscribe, each month you can count on receiving exciting new evidence of God's presence, His guidance and His limitless love for all of us.

Guideposts is also available on the Internet by accessing our home page on the World Wide Web at www.guideposts.org. Send prayer requests to our Monday morning Prayer Fellowship. Read stories from recent issues of our magazines, *Guideposts, Angels on Earth, Clarity, Guideposts for Kids*, and *Guideposts for Teens*, and follow our popular book of daily devotionals, *Daily Guideposts*. Excerpts from some of our best-selling books are also available.